Find Your Leadership Voice in 90 Days

Guided Journal

Find Your Leadership Voice in 90 Days

Guided Journal

KADI COLE

Copyright © 2021 Kadi Cole
All rights reserved.
ISBN: 9798707987199

Cover Design by Pablo Lopez

STAND UP

SPEAK UP

SHOW UP

WITH CONFIDENCE

WELCOME FRIEND!

I am so excited you are diving deep into finding and strengthening your Leadership Voice! This guided journal is designed to develop your self-awareness and lock in your individual learning through reflection, meditation, journaling, and featured exercises. My desire is to enhance your learning, but they are only suggestions!

If God is speaking to you differently or something is not "clicking", don't worry about it. Feel free to use the journal however it best serves you. The goal is for you to reflect and learn, not "follow the rules." There are actually no rules here – just an opportunity for you to hear from God and do what is most helpful!

In the back of this journal, you'll find your Leadership Dashboard. You can also download a PDF version of your Dashboard on our website. As you progress through the next 90 days, be sure to write down what you are learning. By the end you'll have a comprehensive overview of your Leadership Voice and an easy way to stay on track into the future.

This guided journal is part of a bigger system that will help you maximize your growth. You'll benefit the most from it if you also jump into these other components:

- Discover – The *Find Your Leadership Voice in 90 Days* book will guide you through an in-depth study of what your Leadership Voice is and how to use it. This book will add important insight to maximize this guided journal.
- Practice – You can sign up for one year of free weekly emails with short, practical action steps to keep your learnings alive long after you've finished the book.
- Circle Up – The *Circle Up Video Series* gives you my 8 favorite leadership lessons to watch and discussion questions to gather around with a few friends to help you complete your Leadership Voice journey in community.

You can get these resources and more info at FindYourLeadershipVoice.me or KadiCole.com. And I would love to know how this experience is helping you find and use your Leadership Voice – so please reach out at support@kadicole.com and let me know how you are doing and if there's anything I can do to help you!

Cheering you on,

Kadi

DAY 5

Meditate on Ephesians 4:14, "Then we will no longer be infants, tossed back and forth by the waves, and blown here and there..." Write down any reflection or work you need to do in this area.

#FINDYOURLEADERSHIPVOICE

DAY 6

What are the labels you easily go to when judging someone or feeling "less than" yourself?
What are two new, truthful, positive labels you want to start using to describe others? To describe yourself?

#FINDYOURLEADERSHIPVOICE

DAY 7

Am I giving myself the same things I routinely give everyone else I care about? Why or why not?

What do I need to start doing differently to get the most out of this journey to finding my Leadership Voice?

#FINDYOURLEADERSHIPVOICE

DAY 8

Meditate on this verse: "It is the glory of God to conceal a matter; to search out a matter is the glory of kings" Proverbs 25:2 NIV.
List out the items for which you are currently "searching."
Ask God to give you joy in the journey and fun clues to point the way toward discovery.

#FINDYOURLEADERSHIPVOICE

DAY 9

What are your spiritual gifts? Write them down as well as the other skills, talents, and abilities you have seen in yourself. After you've brainstormed a bit, transfer that information to Your Leadership Voice Dashboard at the back of this journal.

#FINDYOURLEADERSHIPVOICE

DAY 10

Are there areas in which you are holding back from using your spiritual gifts? Why?

#FINDYOURLEADERSHIPVOICE

DAY 11

How have you seen or experienced God's anointing? What happened?

#FINDYOURLEADERSHIPVOICE

DAY 12

In what ways you are currently developing your top gifts? Do you use books, mentors, trainings, practicing, or others? What have you learned are some of the burdens of your unique giftings? How do you handle those?

#FINDYOURLEADERSHIPVOICE

DAY 13

How do you normally receive a compliment and why? What prevents you from simply saying "Thank You"? Write out any thoughts or reflections on this.

#FINDYOURLEADERSHIPVOICE

DAY 14

Reflect on Mother Teresa's Quote: "Honesty and transparency make you vulnerable. Be honest and transparent anyway."
How well do you embrace yourself?
Are you comfortable in your own skin? Why or why not?

#FINDYOURLEADERSHIPVOICE

DAY 15

Using the list of potential values below, circle all the values that deeply resonate with you - the ones that are more important than the others. Circle as many as you'd like.
Next, put a star next to the twenty that rise to the top.

- ACCEPTANCE
- ACCESSIBILITY
- ACCOMPLISHMENT
- ACCOUNTABILITY
- ACCURACY
- ACHIEVEMENT
- ACTIVE
- ADAPTABILITY
- ADVENTURE
- AFFECTION
- AGILITY
- ALERTNESS
- ALTRUISM
- AMBITION
- AMUSEMENT
- ANTICIPATE
- APPRECIATION
- APPROACHABLE
- ASSERTIVENESS
- ATTENTIVE
- AUTHENTICITY
- AUTONOMY
- AUTHORITY
- AVAILABLE
- AWARENESS
- BALANCE
- BEAUTY
- BELONGING
- BEST
- BOLDNESS
- BRAVERY
- BRILLIANCE
- CALM
- CANDOR

- CAPABLE
- CAREFUL
- CARING
- CERTAINTY
- CHALLENGE
- CHANGE
- CHARACTER
- CHARITY
- CHEERFUL
- CHILL
- CITIZENSHIP
- CLARITY
- CLEANLINESS
- CLEAR
- CLEVER
- COLLABORATION
- COMFORT
- COMMITMENT
- COMMON SENSE
- COMMUNICATION
- COMMUNITY
- COMPASSION
- COMPETENCY
- COMPETITIVE
- COMPOSURE
- CONCENTRATION
- CONCERN
- CONFIDENCE
- CONFORM
- CONNECTION
- CONSCIOUSNESS
- CONSISTENCY
- CONTENTMENT
- CONTRIBUTION

- CONTROL
- CONVICTION
- COOPERATION
- COORDINATE
- CORRECT
- COURAGE
- COURTESY
- COZY
- CRAFTSMANSHIP
- CREATIVITY
- CREDIBILITY
- CURIOSITY
- DARING
- DECENCY
- DECISIVE
- DEDICATION
- DEPENDABILITY
- DETERMINATION
- DEVELOPMENT
- DEVOTION
- DIFFERENT
- DIGNITY
- DIRECT
- DISCIPLINE
- DISCOVERY
- DIVERSITY
- DREAM
- DRIVE
- DUTY
- EAGER
- ECONOMIC
- EDUCATE
- EFFECTIVE
- EFFICIENCY

DAY 15

- ELEGANCE
- EMPATHY
- EMPOWER
- ENCOURAGE
- ENDURANCE
- ENERGY
- ENGAGEMENT
- ENJOYMENT
- ENTERTAIN
- ENTHUSIASM
- ENTREPRENEURSHIP
- ENVIRONMENT
- EQUALITY
- ETHICAL
- EXCEED
- EXCELLENCE
- EXCITING
- EXPERIENCE
- EXPERTISE
- EXPLORE
- EXPRESSIVE
- FAIRNESS
- FAITH
- FAME
- FAMILY
- FAMOUS
- FAST
- FEARLESS
- FEELINGS
- FEROCIOUS
- FIDELITY
- FITNESS
- FOCUS
- FORESIGHT
- FORTITUDE
- FREEDOM
- FRESH
- FRIENDSHIP
- FRUGAL
- FUN
- GENEROSITY
- GENIUS
- GENIUS
- GIVING
- GOODNESS
- GRACE
- GRATITUDE
- GREATNESS
- GROWTH
- GUIDANCE
- HAPPINESS
- HARD WORK
- HARMONY
- HEALTH HELP
- HOLINESS
- HONESTY
- HONOR
- HOPE
- HOSPITALITY
- HUMILITY
- HUMOR
- HYGIENE
- IMAGINATION
- IMPARTIAL
- IMPROVEMENT
- INDEPENDENCE
- INDIVIDUALITY
- INFLUENCE
- INFORMAL
- INNOVATION
- INQUISITIVE
- INSIGHTFUL
- INSPIRING
- INTEGRITY
- INTERNAL
- INTELLIGENCE
- INTENSITY
- INTENTIONAL
- INTERNATIONAL
- INTUITIVE
- INVENT
- INVEST
- INVITE
- JOY
- JUSTICE
- KINDNESS
- KNOWLEDGE
- LAWFUL
- LEADERSHIP
- LEARNING
- LIBERTY
- LOCAL
- LOGIC
- LONGEVITY
- LOVE
- LOYALTY
- MASTERY
- MATURITY
- MAXIMIZE
- MEANING
- MELLOW
- MEMBERSHIP
- MERIT
- METICULOUS
- MINDFUL
- MODERATION
- MODESTY
- MOTIVATION
- MOVEMENT
- MYSTERY
- NEATNESS
- OBEDIENCE
- OPENNESS
- OPTIMISM
- ORDER
- ORGANIZATION
- ORIGINALITY
- PARTNERSHIP
- PASSION
- PATIENCE
- PEACE
- PEOPLE
- PERFORMANCE
- PERSEVERANCE
- PERSISTENCE
- PERSONAL GROWTH

DAY 15

- PERSUASIVE
- PHYSICAL
- PHILANTHROPY
- PLAYFULNESS
- PLEASANT
- PLEASURE
- POISE
- POPULARITY
- POSITIVE
- POTENTIAL
- POWER
- PRACTICAL
- PRECISE
- PREPARE
- PRESENT
- PRESERVE
- PROCESS
- PRODUCTIVITY
- PROFESSIONALISM
- PROFITABILITY
- PROGRESS
- PROSPERITY
- PUNCTUAL
- PURITY
- PURPOSE
- PURSUE
- QUALITY
- RATIONAL
- REAL
- REALISTIC
- REASON
- RECOGNITION
- RECREATION
- REFLECTION
- RELATIONSHIPS
- RELAX
- RELIABLE
- RELIGION
- REPUTATION
- RESILIENT
- RESOLVE
- RESOURCEFUL
- RESPECT
- RESPONSIBILITY
- REST
- RESTRAINT
- RESULTS
- REVERENCE
- RIGOR
- RISK
- SACRIFICE
- SAFETY
- SATISFACTION
- SECURITY
- SELF-AWARENESS
- SELFLESS
- SENSITIVITY
- SERENITY
- SERIOUS
- SERVICE
- SHARING
- SIGNIFICANCE
- SILENCE
- SILLINESS
- SIMPLICITY
- SINCERITY
- SKILL
- SKILLFULNESS
- SMART
- SOLITUDE
- SPIRIT
- SPIRITUALITY
- SPONTANEOUS
- STABILITY
- STATUS
- STEALTH
- STEWARDSHIP
- STRENGTH
- STRUCTURE
- SUCCESS
- SUPPORT
- SURPRISE
- SUSTAINABILITY
- SYMPATHY
- SYNERGY
- SYSTEMS
- TALENT
- TEAMWORK
- THANKFUL
- THOROUGH
- THOUGHTFUL
- TIMELINESS
- TOLERANCE
- TOUGHNESS
- TRADITIONAL
- TRAINING
- TRANQUILITY
- TRANSPARENCY
- TRUST
- TRUSTWORTHINESS
- TRUTH
- UNDERSTANDING
- UNIQUENESS
- UNITY
- UNIVERSAL
- USEFULNESS
- UTILITY
- VALOR
- VALUE
- VARIETY
- VIBRANT
- VICTORY
- VIGOR
- VISION
- VITALITY
- WARMTH
- WEALTH
- WELCOMING
- WILLING
- WINNING
- WISDOM
- WONDER

DAY 16

Transfer your Top 20 starred values from yesterday's list.

MY TOP 20 VALUES

#FINDYOURLEADERSHIPVOICE

DAY 16

Now it's time to refine your list - which ones are similar or overlap? How can you combine, rename, or even add a word that captures the essence of the value you are identifying? Ask for help from people who know you well and can help you. Keep in mind values are not aspirational - these need to be values that you are *consistently* and *currently* living out.

Your goal is to prune the list until you have 3-10 final personal leadership values that represent how you use your Leadership Voice in a way that is *authentically* you.

When you have settled on your list, transfer them to your Leadership Dashboard in the back of this journal.

MY PERSONAL LEADERSHIP VALUES

#FINDYOURLEADERSHIPVOICE

DAY 17

Have you found your "tribe" yet?
List out the people with whom you share many similar values.
Do they reflect the diversity of every tribe, tongue, and nation?
What is one area in which you want to start building or expanding your tribe?

#FINDYOURLEADERSHIPVOICE

DAY 18

How do you tend to get caught up in perfectionism? Name a couple examples of when this has happened to you and how it affected you?

#FINDYOURLEADERSHIPVOICE

DAY 19

When you think of your "passions," what usually comes to mind? Are they a "who" or a "what"?

#FINDYOURLEADERSHIPVOICE

DAY 20

Brainstorm all the groups of people that might be your passion. Whittle them down to any one or two common denominators and write them on Your Leadership Voice Dashboard in the back of this journal.

#FINDYOURLEADERSHIPVOICE

DAY 21

Take a look at your Leadership Dashboard, then reflect and journal: Which do you have the most clarity around – your values, your talents, or your passion?
Which is the least clear? Do you have an imbalance anywhere?

#FINDYOURLEADERSHIPVOICE

DAY 22

Are you walking your own path? Are there temptations on the wide, common road that you need to surrender?

#FINDYOURLEADERSHIPVOICE

DAY 23

Meditate on this verse for a few minutes: "For if you remain silent at this time, relief and deliverance will arise...from another place... And who knows but that you have come to your royal position for such a time as this?" Esther 4:14 NIV.

Are there any areas God is revealing to you in which you are remaining silent when you have been positioned to speak?

#FINDYOURLEADERSHIPVOICE

DAY 24

What is your relationship with authority?
Do you consider it something good and helpful, or does it bring up memories of when people have abused their authority?

#FINDYOURLEADERSHIPVOICE

DAY 25

Take a moment to pray.
Ask God to open up your heart to fully see and embrace the authority He has already given you. Write out your prayer.

#FINDYOURLEADERSHIPVOICE

DAY 26

Are you leading yourself well? Are you in control of the things in your life that God has given you personal authority over, such as what you eat, what you say, how you spend your free time, your health, your finances, your relationships, and your connection with Him? What is God inviting you to change?

#FINDYOURLEADERSHIPVOICE

DAY 27

Write down your thoughts to the following questions:
Do you struggle to feel approved by God?
Do you worry you could lose His approval?
How can you lead and speak as if you already have straight A's (*which you do*) and will never again start at zero?

#FINDYOURLEADERSHIPVOICE

DAY 28

How skilled are you at setting and keeping boundaries? Why? What physical reaction happens in your body when someone violates a boundary you have set?

#FINDYOURLEADERSHIPVOICE

DAY 29

How are you at respecting other peoples' boundaries? Where could you use some accountability in honoring other peoples' boundaries better?

#FINDYOURLEADERSHIPVOICE

DAY 30

What step can you take today to begin exercising the spiritual authority you already have?
Pray and ask God to send you an opportunity and see what He brings you today!

#FINDYOURLEADERSHIPVOICE

DAY 31

Spend some time meditating on the following verse: "For God has not given us a spirit of fear, but of power and of love and of a sound mind" 2 Timothy 1:6-7 NKJV.

Are there areas in which you struggle with fear more than others? Write out a prayer to God telling Him about those struggles and asking for His help.

#FINDYOURLEADERSHIPVOICE

DAY 32

Make a list of all the Little 'a' Agenda items that are on your plate right now. Then, write out some of the Big 'A' Agenda items God has "interrupted" your day with in the past. Take a moment to thank Him for those opportunities, and then surrender your Little 'a' Agenda priorities for today to Him and His bigger "A" Agenda.

#FINDYOURLEADERSHIPVOICE

DAY 33

What challenges you or tempts you about power?
Are you attracted to it or do you avoid it? Write about a time you handled power incorrectly and what you learned.

#FINDYOURLEADERSHIPVOICE

DAY 34

Spend some time meditating on Romans 13:1: "...There is no authority except that which God has established..."
Write down all the areas over which God has given you authority - personally, spiritually, organizationally, and within your family. Write out a prayer of thanksgiving for all the people God has given you influence.
Ask Him for His help in stewarding that well today.

#FINDYOURLEADERSHIPVOICE

DAY 35

Where are you shrinking back? Are you getting caught in the Likability Trap?
What could help you from doing this?

#FINDYOURLEADERSHIPVOICE

DAY 36

What kind of plate are you using right now?
A salad plate, turkey platter, or tiered cake stand? What do you need to start delegating, outsourcing, or asking for help with?

#FINDYOURLEADERSHIPVOICE

DAY 37

Think through Parker Palmer's statement, "A leader is someone with the power to project either shadow or light onto some part of the world and onto the lives of the people who dwell there. A leader shapes the ethos in which others must live, an ethos as light-filled as heaven or as shadowy as hell. A good leader is intensely aware of the interplay of inner shadow and light, lest the act of leadership do more harm than good."

Journal any reflections you have on this.

#FINDYOURLEADERSHIPVOICE

DAY 38

Are you withholding good from anyone? Are you growing weary in doing good towards someone? Why? Who do you need to approach differently to truly invest in their development this week?

#FINDYOURLEADERSHIPVOICE

DAY 39

Meditate on Ecclesiastes 3:7 NIV: "[There is] a time to be silent and a time to speak." Do you need to work more on staying silent or speaking up? Why?

#FINDYOURLEADERSHIPVOICE

DAY 40

Have you ever been called to use your Leadership Voice to speak to those with more power than you?
Do you sense God calling you to do it now?
What can you learn from the Daughters of Zelophehad?

#FINDYOURLEADERSHIPVOICE

DAY 41

Meditate on this verse:
"...Do not worry beforehand about what to say." Mark 13:11 NIV. Think of a time when God gave you exactly what to say in the moment it was needed. Where do you need God to help you with your words today? Pray and ask Him for help, and then trust that He will be with you - whatever you face today.

#FINDYOURLEADERSHIPVOICE

DAY 42

Giving ourselves permission to practice, make mistakes, learn, and try again is important when determining where our authority begins and ends. How kind are you with yourself when you are learning? How can you give yourself permission to practice using your Leadership Voice?

#FINDYOURLEADERSHIPVOICE

DAY 43

What are some of the different ways God speaks to you? List out what they are and how you knew it was God. What can you learn from this list?

#FINDYOURLEADERSHIPVOICE

DAY 44

How well do you express yourself? What is it you usually regret? In what way do you hope to get better? Ask God to help you.

#FINDYOURLEADERSHIPVOICE

DAY 45

List out any negative or untrue statements that continue to pop into your mind when you think about expressing your Leadership Voice. Next, list out truths from God's Word that cancels out each of those lies (*Google if you need to*).
And finally, write down some of the positive feedback you've received from coworkers, peers, mentors, friends, and family.

Negative or Untrue Statements	Corresponding Truths From God's Word

POSITIVE FEEDBACK YOU'VE GOTTEN:

DAY 46

When you think of using your Leadership Voice, what thoughts enter your head? Do you celebrate your courage, or do you get hit with judgement and criticism?
Write out a prayer asking God to help you renew your mind with His truth about your Leadership Voice.

#FINDYOURLEADERSHIPVOICE

DAY 47

Is your natural tendency to be over-prepared or to wing it? How has this been helpful to you in the past, and what have been the downsides? What do you need to do to operate in the healthy middle more often?

DAY 48

What are your most helpful practices for preparing your content, your internal mindset, and your spirit?

If you've never identified these before, take some time to write them out and decide what works best for you.

Are there any practices you need to add to be better prepared?

Are there any bad habits that aren't serving you well?

#FINDYOURLEADERSHIPVOICE

DAY 49

Write out what places and people you have in your life right now that are safe for you to practice growing your Leadership Voice.
Is it time to ask if they'll let you practice on them?
Is there anyone you need to add to your circle?

#FINDYOURLEADERSHIPVOICE

DAY 50

Who can you advocate for today? Is it someone in a meeting, at the dinner table, or even someone you see at the store?
Ask God for opportunities to stand up for other's Leadership Voices as well as your own.

#FINDYOURLEADERSHIPVOICE

DAY 51

Are you someone who naturally sees what's wrong or do you naturally see solutions? Write down some challenges you are facing right now. What are some possible solutions?
Ask God to help open your mind and heart to the possibilities He has for those situations.

#FINDYOURLEADERSHIPVOICE

DAY 52

Spend some time meditating on this verse:
"A person finds joy in giving an apt reply - and how good is a timely word!" Proverbs 15:23 NIV.
How well do you give a timely reply?
Are you paying attention throughout your day to be able to seize the opportunity to use your Leadership Voice?

#FINDYOURLEADERSHIPVOICE

DAY 53

Which side do you naturally communicate from – your head or your heart? How has using only one side limited your Leadership Voice? What can you start doing to build up the side that is missing from your Leadership Voice?

#FINDYOURLEADERSHIPVOICE

DAY 54

How well do your words express what you really think or feel?
What "go to" phrases or habits do you tend to hide behind, such as apologies, too many thank yous, emojis, or non-committal language?
What can you do to start moving toward speaking more truthfully?

#FINDYOURLEADERSHIPVOICE

DAY 55

How do you feel about your appearance? Are you thinking about it too much, not enough, or just right?
Does your appearance match your Leadership Voice?
If not, what could you do to bring them into alignment?

#FINDYOURLEADERSHIPVOICE

DAY 56

Do you regularly receive constructive feedback? If so, write down some of the helpful things you've learned from that feedback.
If not, what steps do you need to take to invite more helpful and constructive feedback into your Leadership Voice?

#FINDYOURLEADERSHIPVOICE

DAY 57

What is your relationship with fear? Does it grip you and make you powerless, or have you learned some ways to conquer it?
Spend some time reflecting on what you've learned through the years and how you can walk in less fear.

#FINDYOURLEADERSHIPVOICE

DAY 58

Meditate on this verse: "For God has not given us a spirit of fear, but of power and of love and of a sound mind" 2 Timothy 1:7 NKJV. Then Pray OUT LOUD: "God has not given me a spirit of fear. Instead, He has given me a spirit of power and of love and of a sound mind by the blood of Jesus. Amen."
Repeat, and let it sink into your spirit.

#FINDYOURLEADERSHIPVOICE

DAY 59

What characteristics do you have of the Superwoman Syndrome? Stretched too thin, lots on your mind, feel like a failure, difficulty saying 'no,' stressed, difficulty taking a true vacation?
What is this costing you?
What deeper fear might be behind those limitations?
What's the truth from God that dispels that fear?

#FINDYOURLEADERSHIPVOICE

#FINDYOURLEADERSHIPVOICE

DAY 61

Meditate on this verse: "God did not send His Son into the world to condemn the world, but to save the world through Him. Whoever believes in Him is not condemned" John 3:17-18. NIV

Write out the condemning thoughts or "voices in your head" that are not from God. Then write out what God *does* think about you. Pray and ask God to replace those negative voices with His truth.

#FINDYOURLEADERSHIPVOICE

DAY 62

On the left side of the page, right down all the "what if's" that are floating in your mind. On the right side, turn that statement into an "even if" statement. Work to find an "even if" for every "what if."

#FINDYOURLEADERSHIPVOICE

DAY 63

Read through John 17.
Write down, in your own words, Jesus' vision for unity.
Pray and ask God to use you to build a Together Culture today.

#FINDYOURLEADERSHIPVOICE

DAY 64

Do you naturally lean toward togetherness or competition?
Have you ever struggled with a case of "niceness" that limited your Leadership Voice?
How have you seen a win:win mindset work for everyone?

#FINDYOURLEADERSHIPVOICE

DAY 65

We are responsible for building trust in 360 degrees of our Leadership Voice — with the leaders above you, those working alongside you, and those you lead. With whom do you need to have a trust-building conversation? Take some time to write out what you could say to them to deal with the issue directly and honestly, but also to build trust relationally.

#FINDYOURLEADERSHIPVOICE

DAY 66

How well do you connect through conversations? Is it usually a 50-50 exchange, or do you find yourself dominating or deferring too much? What is behind that inclination, and how can you shift to have more equitable interactions with people?

#FINDYOURLEADERSHIPVOICE

DAY 67

Look Backwards - How have I been using my Leadership Voice to feel important or loved? When have I felt desperate or the need to prove myself? What were the results in me, my relationships, and productivity?

Look Forward - How can I start moving from desperation to curiosity? Where is an opportunity for me to share my perspective rather than try to prove myself?

#FINDYOURLEADERSHIPVOICE

DAY 68

Do you feel like you are right on time? What do you need to accept and surrender about yourself? How can you better embrace where you are on your journey, trusting that God has been directing your steps for His greater purpose in you?

#FINDYOURLEADERSHIPVOICE

DAY 69

Write out your experience with the Mirror Exercise.
What have you learned about yourself?

#FINDYOURLEADERSHIPVOICE

DAY 70

What does it look like when you get *WHO* you are (*your value*) and *WHAT* you do (*your performance*) right?
Think through this and list out your early warning signs that these are getting mixed up in your heart.

#FINDYOURLEADERSHIPVOICE

DAY 71

Spend some time meditating on Psalm 55, when King David was betrayed by a close friend. Write down any thoughts or experiences you've had that are similar to this.

#FINDYOURLEADERSHIPVOICE

DAY 72

Meditate on this verse: "Follow justice and justice alone, so that you may live and possess the land the Lord your God is giving you" Deuteronomy 16:20 NIV. Where is there injustice around you? Is there anything you need to speak up for and make right?

#FINDYOURLEADERSHIPVOICE

DAY 73

When have you felt your Leadership Voice was silenced by others? What was that like for you? Do you have any forgiveness to work through? Write about it here.

#FINDYOURLEADERSHIPVOICE

DAY 74

How have you handled put-downs in the past?
What would be a better response that is more in line with your Leadership Voice?

#FINDYOURLEADERSHIPVOICE

DAY 75

Spend some time meditating on this verse: "Do not take to heart all the things that people say" Ecclesiastes 7:21 ESV. How do you normally respond to feeling judged? How can you work to let go of other peoples' opinions and live for an audience of One?

#FINDYOURLEADERSHIPVOICE

DAY 76

Is there a relationship or a work situation that you are holding onto too tightly? Why? How might God be able to use your Leadership Voice if you were to let go?

#FINDYOURLEADERSHIPVOICE

DAY 77

How integrated are your heart-soul-mind-strength?
Is there any part of yourself that you often compartmentalize or shrink back from?

#FINDYOURLEADERSHIPVOICE

DAY 78

Where do you tend to get triggered? Write down some responses in your heart-soul-mind-strength when you experience this? What helps pull you out of it?

#FINDYOURLEADERSHIPVOICE

DAY 79

What are your favorite ways to worship God with your integrated heart-soul-mind-strength?

#FINDYOURLEADERSHIPVOICE

DAY 80

What have you found works for you to rest your heart-soul-mind-strength? Why do you think that works for you?
What would you like to try next?

#FINDYOURLEADERSHIPVOICE

DAY 81

How is your posture? Does it adequately reflect the strength and flexibility of the Leadership Voice God has given you?

#FINDYOURLEADERSHIPVOICE

DAY 82

What physical and mental health rhythms are you keeping up with well? Do you need to add any into your routine?

#FINDYOURLEADERSHIPVOICE

DAY 83

How do you feel about your physical voice? What kind of feedback have you gotten about it from others? Is there anything you'd like to work on to be more in control of your voice and have it more accurately reflect your Leadership Voice?

#FINDYOURLEADERSHIPVOICE

DAY 84

Meditate on this verse: "I cry out with my whole heart"
Psalm 119:145 NKJV.
Think through the last time you really cried. How did it help?
Is there anything you are holding back from crying about? Why?
When will you give yourself time and space to cry?

#FINDYOURLEADERSHIPVOICE

DAY 85

How have you seen the temptation to vent show up in your life and leadership? What are better ways you can assertively solve the situation using your strong and courageous Leadership Voice, rather than hiding behind venting?

#FINDYOURLEADERSHIPVOICE

DAY 86

Think through the dimensions of your heart-soul-mind-strength. What actions or activities do you enjoy that hit on all four of those at once? How can you make it easier for yourself to release any negative energy or emotions in one of these ways rather than in harmful "quick fixes"?

#FINDYOURLEADERSHIPVOICE

DAY 87

Who has left an impact on you through the legacy of their Leadership Voice? Write out their names here. Thank God for their role in your life and consider sending them a note or giving them a call to let them know.

#FINDYOURLEADERSHIPVOICE

DAY 88

How much have you thought about the time and place in history in which God has positioned you? What is special about *now* that God would insert your unique Leadership Voice? Is there anything you need to do to gain a better understanding of our times?

#FINDYOURLEADERSHIPVOICE

DAY 89

Whose Leadership Voice are you actively championing? Write down their names and how you see them responding to your investment. Who do you need to add to that list? Is there anyone that needs to come off of the list?

#FINDYOURLEADERSHIPVOICE

DAY 90

Who has God called you to speak up for? How can you start helping someone else's Leadership Voice be heard?
Stop and thank God for how He is using your Leadership Voice, and for the legacy He is building in and through you.

#FINDYOURLEADERSHIPVOICE

NO MORE WAFFLING
NO MORE WONDERING
NO MORE QUESTIONING

MY LEADERSHIP

WHAT TO SAY — My God-given spiritual gifts and abilities	**HOW** TO SAY IT — My personal leadership values
• • • • • •	• • • • • •

WHO TO SPEAK UP FOR — My individual passions and callings

-
-
-

WHEN TO SPEAK — What authority have I been given?

Personal	Family
• • •	• • •
Spiritual	Organizational
• • •	• • •

VOICE DASHBOARD

THE FOUNDATION
What do I need to remember about my identity in Christ?

-
-
-
-
-

BEING PRESENT & CONFIDENT
Ways I need to nurture and integrate my heart-soul-mind-strength

-
-
-
-
-

MY REMINDERS
Important learnings for me to keep in mind

-
-
-
-
-

KADICOLE
& company

- EXECUTIVE COACHING
- LEADERSHIP COURSES
- SPEAKING
- LIFE PLANS

Visit KadiCole.com for more information

ABOUT THE AUTHOR

Known for her strategic insight and thought leadership, Kadi Cole has spent the last 30 years serving in various leadership roles including University Dean and Executive Director at one of America's largest and fastest growing multi-site churches. Specializing in building leadership development systems across multiple locations, Kadi is an international consultant for businesses and non- profits as they scale their growth, cultivate healthy cultures, and develop the leadership potential within their organization including overcoming barriers for minority team members.

Kadi is a best-selling author, speaker, leadership trainer, executive coach, and Life Plan facilitator. She holds a master's degree in Human Resource Development focusing on transformational education, and a bachelor's degree in Nursing with expertise in College/Adolescent Health and Mental Health. You can find Kadi on social media **@kadicole**, hiking the mountains in her home state of Montana, or enjoying the dog beach in South Florida where she lives with her family.

To learn more about Kadi's services or invite her to speak, please visit **KadiCole.com**.

KADI COLE'S
FIND YOUR LEADERSHIP VOICE
EXPERIENCE

Find Your Leadership Voice in 90 Days Book

Learn how to speak, up, show up, and stand out with confidence.

Circle Up Video Series

Eight new leadership lessons to complement your learnings from the book. Gather with a few friends and talk through the accompanying questions to complete your Leadership Voice journey in community.

Guided Journal

Daily reflection prompts to help develop your self-awareness and lock in your individual learning.

Action Emails

One year of free weekly emails with short, practical action steps to keep your learnings alive long after you've finished the book.

Learn more at FindYourLeadershipVoice.me

Made in the USA
Las Vegas, NV
05 June 2025